COLONIAL AMERICA

by

Marci Appelbaum and Jeff Catanese

■ SCHOLASTIC
Teaching
Resources

New York • Toronto • London
Auckland • Sydney • Mexico City
New Delhi • Hong Kong • Buenos Aires

Jeff would like to dedicate this book to his mom and dad, his first teachers.

To Mom, Dad and Cindy with love—MA

Edited by Sarah Glasscock
Cover art and interior illustrations by Mona Mark
Cover design by Gerard Fuchs
Interior design by Melinda Belter
ISBN: 0-439-36602-X

1 2 3 4 5 6 7 8 9 10   40   09 08 07 06 05 04 03

CONTENTS

INTRODUCTION

How did the American colonies get started, and what was life like for the colonists? What was the first Thanksgiving really about? How did the growth of the triangle trade impact the early American economy? Why were people in Salem accused of witchcraft and put on trial? How have the events of this period impacted American life today?

Read-Aloud Plays: Colonial America invites students to explore the intriguing characters, pivotal events, and critical issues of this formative period of American history. These five original plays present an overview of the American colonial period—the development and eventual demise of Jamestown, the story of the first Thanksgiving and its relationship to the holiday we know today, the far-reaching impact of the triangle trade and slavery, the political and social corruption surrounding the Salem witch trials, and the similarities and differences among English, French, and Spanish colonies.

DESCRIPTION OF THE TEACHING GUIDES

This collection of plays and supporting material is designed to enrich your existing social studies curriculum. Each play is followed by background information on the events, a resource section of book and Web links, and related activities. The activities emphasize critical thinking about historical issues through discussion, writing, and researching. They promote individual work as well as cooperative learning. Feel free to adjust the activity plans to meet the particular needs and interests of your students.

PRESENTING THE PLAYS

The plays support a variety of instructional purposes—from teaching historical concepts to building teamwork in a cooperative production. Presenting the plays in a particular format will help you match your objective. For example, you might use a play to kick off a lesson. An informal read-through of *Four Homes* can prepare students for a discussion on daily life in the American colonies and for other related activities. However, you and your students may want to present a fully staged class play like *What Happened Here?* so that they may more thoroughly understand the events surrounding the trials. You can involve students in cooperative work to cast, rehearse, research, and create costumes and props for their production.

Opportunities for learning increase as more students become involved in the plays, so it is important to help all students find ways to get into the act, either on stage or behind the scenes! In many instances you may change the male roles to female roles and vice versa, as needed. You may also want to encourage nontraditional casting. Students who are not comfortable performing can take on important roles offstage as set and costume designers, props managers, and researchers.

What better way to learn about the past and present than to participate in the drama of history? By lending their own voices and experiences to the production of these plays, your students will have a chance to interact with events and people that have helped to shape America and make important connections with the world today.

WHO WANTS TO BE A COLONIST?

—

The Jamestown Settlement

CHARACTERS
(in order of appearance)

ANNOUNCER

AUDIENCE

REGIS HISTORY: *game show host*

DR. JOE: *a contestant*

FRED THE COLONIST: *a contestant*

KING JAMES I: *King of England*

ENGLISH GENTLEMAN

COLONIST 1 • COLONIST 2 • COLONIST 3

COLONIST 4 • COLONIST 5

Read-Aloud Plays: Colonial America • Scholastic Teaching Resources

SETTING: *The set of a modern-day television game show*

ANNOUNCER: Ladies and gentlemen, it's time for your favorite game show and mine . . . *Who Wants to Be a Colonist?*!

Audience cheers. TV game show theme music plays.
Host, Regis History, runs in. More cheers.

REGIS: Welcome! Welcome, everyone. I'm Regis History. And this is *Who Wants to Be a Colonist?* This week's topic is . . . Jamestown!

Audience cheers.

REGIS: With the help of our two contestants, we'll learn all about the Jamestown settlement and whether or not it succeeded. But before we begin the game, let's meet our wonderful contestants!

    Our first contestant comes to us from modern-day Virginia. He's a dentist whose hobbies include coin collecting and appearing on game shows. Please, let's welcome Dr. Joe Johnson!

Joe runs onstage and takes his place behind a podium.
Audience cheers.

REGIS: Our second contestant has traveled all the way from the year 1608 to be with us. He's a down-and-out Englishman trying to make his way in the New World. His interests include hiding from the Powhatan and escaping disease. Please welcome Fred the Colonist, from Jamestown!

Fred runs onstage and takes his place behind a podium.
Audience cheers.

REGIS: Okay, contestants, here's how to play the game. You'll watch a series of scenes about Jamestown and then I'll ask you questions about the scenes. Okay, let's play *Who Wants to Be a Colonist?*

Audience cheers.

ANNOUNCER: Scene One: A group of Englishmen ask for permission to go to the New World.

King James and English Gentleman enter.

GENTLEMAN: . . . and that's why we want to establish a colony in the New World, Your Majesty.

KING JAMES: Hmmmm . . . very interesting.

GENTLEMAN: Do you really think so?

KING JAMES: I think this could be a very good opportunity for England, so I'll help you. I'll form a company that's chartered to colonize the New World. You and your friends can represent the company and set up a colony over there. I'll even give you three boats to sail over on.

GENTLEMAN: Thank you, Your Majesty!

Gentleman and King James bow and exit. Audience cheers.

REGIS: Here's your first question: What year was that?

FRED: Buzz! That was 1606—we landed in 1607.

REGIS: That's correct. Here's your next question: What was the name of the king you just saw?

FRED: Buzz! King James the First.

REGIS: Correct again! That's two correct answers for Fred the Colonist and no correct answers for Dr. Joe.

JOE: Well, this really isn't fair. He was there! I just read about it in a history book. Of course it's easier for him to remember something like 1606—it was practically yesterday for him!

REGIS: Now Joe, be a good sport. Maybe you'll do better on our next question. Hands on buzzers. What were the names of the three ships sanctioned by King James to sail for the New World?

JOE: Buzz! I know this one! The *Nina,* the *Pinta,* and the *Santa María*!

REGIS: Oh! I'm sorry, Joe, but that is incorrect. The *Nina, Pinta,* and *Santa María* were Christopher Columbus's ships, which sailed in 1492. The ships that set out for the new world in 1606 were the *Susan Constant,* the *Discovery,* and the *Godspeed.*

FRED: I knew that! I knew that! I was on board the *Discovery*! *(He holds his stomach like he is going to be sick.)* What a ride that was! We spent weeks at sea.

JOE: This is *so* not fair!

REGIS: Next question. What was the name of the English company formed to colonize the New World for the English?

FRED: Buzz! The Virginia Company of London! And when the Virginia Company was formed, King James gave us permission to set up a colony in the New World.

REGIS: Nice job, Fred. And for an extra point, can you tell me what kind of company the Virginia Company of London was?

Read-Aloud Plays: Colonial America • Scholastic Teaching Resources

FRED: It was a joint-stock company, Regis.

REGIS: Excellent.

JOE: What in the world is a joint-stock company?

FRED: It's a way that a new colony can get set up. It's when a group of merchants pays for an expedition. For example, we were given money to go to the New World and build up the area and work there. Then we sent the resources from the New World back to England. The merchants who gave us the money to begin with sold the resources that we sent back and made lots of money.

REGIS: That's an excellent explanation, Fred. Now here's the final question about this scene. Give three reasons why the English wanted to settle in the New World.

JOE: Aaah! I know! I know! Buzz! Because it was really cool!

REGIS: Oh, that is really wrong. I am so sorry, but "because it was really cool" is not a good enough answer. The correct answer is . . .

JOE: Wait! I really do know! They wanted religious freedom.

REGIS: Well, Joe, that is a much better answer than "because it was really cool," but you are still incorrect. Other colonies were formed because the settlers wanted religious freedom, but that was not the case with Jamestown.

FRED: Buzz! We wanted to go to the New World to find gold!

REGIS: And?

FRED: And we wanted to improve trade to the New World . . . uh . . . and we wanted to prevent the Spanish from settling all of the New World themselves.

REGIS: Great answers, Fred! I would also have accepted that the English wanted to find a new water route to China. The score is now four points for Fred the Colonist and zero for Dr. Joe. Let's move onto our next scene.

ANNOUNCER: Scene Two: English colonists land in the New World.

Colonists 1, 2, and 3 enter and look around.

COLONIST 1: Hey, I think this would be a great spot to build a fort!

COLONIST 2: Here? You've got to be kidding.

COLONIST 1: What's wrong with this spot? I think it's perfect! I mean, it's right by the water and all . . .

COLONIST 3: You really want to set up a fort right here?

COLONIST 1: Yes. Right here. I think our colony would really thrive right here!

Colonists bow and exit. Audience cheers.

REGIS: Nice job, colonists. Excellent scene. Contestants, here's your first question in round two. Why did the colonists choose this inland location along the James River?

FRED: Buzz! First of all, it was protected on three sides by the river and marshes, so it had strong military advantages. It was also far away from the Spanish settlements, so we wouldn't have to worry about being attacked by the Spaniards.

REGIS: That's correct. Next question. Why was this location a bad choice?

FRED: Buzz! I know this one! I was there! Ugh. We all got sick. There was plenty of water, but no fresh water. We had to drink the same water we threw our waste in and so we got dysentery. Have you ever seen a room full of people with dysentery? *(Holding his nose)* Believe me, you don't want to.

REGIS: All right, Fred. I would have also accepted that the marshy land wasn't good for growing crops. Let's move on to the next scene.

ANNOUNCER: Scene Three: The colonists meet their neighbors.

Colonists 4 and 5 enter and hide behind a tree to listen for attackers.

COLONIST 4: Did you hear that?

COLONIST 5: What?

COLONIST 4: That noise. In the bushes. Didn't you hear it?

COLONIST 5: No. What do you think it was?

COLONIST 4: There it is again. It sounds like . . . it sounds like . . .

Both colonists "see" something offstage and begin screaming.
Finally they stop and take a bow. Audience cheers.

REGIS: All right. That was pretty scary. Here comes your question. The colonists you just saw were frightened when they saw members of a certain Indian tribe. What Indian tribe did the colonists of Jamestown encounter?

FRED: Buzz! The Powhatans!

REGIS: Correct! Next question: How did the colonists and the Powhatans get along with one another?

FRED: Buzz! They wouldn't leave us alone!

REGIS: That's incorrect, Fred. I think you could use a little perspective on this question. The correct answer is that the English settled on land already inhabited by the Powhatans. The colonists moved in without finding out if anyone already occupied the land. This, of course, angered the Powhatans, who feared being run off their own land. There were also many cultural differences between the English and the Powhatans.

FRED: Gee, I never thought about it that way.

REGIS: Now, let's see our final scene.

ANNOUNCER: Scene Four: The colonists have a hard time at Jamestown.

Colonists 1, 2, and 3 enter looking cold and miserable. Some lie on the ground, as if dead.

COLONIST 1: I am *so* cold!

COLONIST 2: I am *so* cold and *so* hungry!

COLONIST 3: I am *so* cold and *so* hungry and . . .

*Colonist 3 falls to the ground. Colonists bow and exit.
Audience cheers.*

REGIS: Thank you, colonists, that was excellent. Now contestants, here's your first question. What is going on in this scene?

FRED: Buzz! I object! This scene never happened in Jamestown. I mean, we've been cold and sick, and people have died, but not like that.

REGIS: Oh, sorry Fred. That's incorrect.

JOE: I know! Buzz! That's the "starving time"!

FRED: The "starving time"? What are you talking about?

JOE: The winter when over 400 colonists died from cold, illness, or starvation.

FRED: Over 400 died? Don't you think I would remember that?

REGIS: Not necessarily, Fred. That leads us to our next question. In what year did the "starving time" happen?

JOE: Buzz! 1609.

REGIS: That's correct. Nice comeback, Joe.

FRED: 1609? That's what's going to happen to us just next year?

REGIS: Sorry, Fred. Now you understand why you couldn't recognize the action in that scene. You come to us from 1608, so you won't experience the "starving time" for another year. But don't you worry about that right now—It's time to play the lightning round!

Audience cheers.

REGIS: Hands on your buzzers, contestants. Who was the first leader of Jamestown?

FRED: Buzz! John Smith?

REGIS: Correct. Who was considered to be a hero for improving relations with the Powhatan?

JOE: Buzz! Fred the Colonist?

REGIS: Incorrect. The answer again is Captain John Smith. Who was the Indian princess who may have saved John Smith's life? Her story later became a popular cartoon.

JOE: Buzz! The little mermaid!

REGIS: No, Joe, I'm sorry. The correct answer is Pocahontas. How many women were living in Jamestown in 1607?

FRED: Buzz! None.

REGIS: Correct. Here's your follow-up question: When did women arrive in Jamestown?

JOE: Buzz! After 1607!

REGIS: That is correct, Joe, but not specific enough. The exact answer is 1609.

FRED: There are going to be women in Jamestown soon?

REGIS: Women and children will arrive, but so will more hard times, disease, starvation, and death. Next question: What was the most important crop grown in Jamestown?

FRED: Crop? We finally got crops to grow?

REGIS: You certainly did. John Rolfe began growing tobacco in 1612. Tobacco is the answer I was looking for.

FRED: Tobacco? Why was tobacco an important crop?

Read-Aloud Plays: Colonial America • Scholastic Teaching Resources

REGIS: In 1614 the first shipment of Virginia tobacco was sold in London. Tobacco was a big hit.

JOE: No kidding. Jamestown sold tobacco all over the world.

REGIS: Right. But Jamestown's industry was still controlled by England. All sales of tobacco had to go through London, so England's treasury kept most of the profit. Eventually, the fact that the colonists weren't allowed to sell tobacco directly to other countries without going through England helped start the Revolutionary War.

FRED: The Revolutionary War? Yipes! What is that?

JOE: Only THE most important war in our country's history—the American Revolution.

FRED: I'm an English colonist—what do I know about an American revolution? Where's America? I didn't even know about tobacco or women in Jamestown after 1608. This game is not fair at all.

REGIS: Let's move on. We have one final question. When were the Virginia Company of London and the Jamestown settlement finally dissolved?

FRED: Dissolved? Jamestown was dissolved?

JOE: Of course it was dissolved. Do you still see the Jamestown settlement around today? Does anyone ever say "I'm driving to the Jamestown settlement to get some groceries?"

FRED: How should I know about that? What do you think I am, a soothsayer?

JOE: Maybe you are. I mean, you managed to travel here from the past, didn't you?

*Joe and Fred continue to argue. They lower their voices but move
as if they are having a big argument.*

REGIS: Okay, contestants, I'll repeat the question one more time. When were the Virginia Company of London and the Jamestown Settlement dissolved? . . . Anyone? *(Looks to contestants, who continue to argue and then back to audience)* The correct answer is in the 1620s. The Virginia Company of London was dissolved in the late 1620s and the Jamestown Settlement eventually became a part of Virginia. And that's all the time we have for today! I'd like to thank our contestants, Joe and Fred. Join us next week on *Who Wants to Be a Colonist?* when we take you to Salem to figure out which contestant is really a witch! Thank you, and good night everyone!

Music comes back up. Joe and Fred argue louder. Audience cheers.

Read-Aloud Plays: Colonial America • Scholastic Teaching Resources

BACKGROUND ON JAMESTOWN

The Jamestown settlement in Virginia was founded in 1607 when King James I sent men from England to the New World to settle land there. Over 100 men set out on three ships, the *Godspeed,* the *Discovery,* and the *Susan Constant* so that they might lay claim to part of the New World for England. King James had very specific interests in the New World. He was hoping to find gold there for England. He also wanted to improve trade to the New World, find a better water route to China, and prevent the Spaniards from settling all of the New World on their own.

Upon arriving in what is now Virginia, the settlers chose an unfortunate spot along the marshy banks of a river known to the native Indians as "Powhatan's Flu." The Englishmen renamed it the "James" after their king. They thought that the location, surrounded by water on three sides, would allow fewer opportunities for attacks on the fort by other settlers and thus have strong military advantages. However, the banks of the river proved to be a poor choice. Crops did not grow well in the extreme dampness of the marshland, and the settlers developed dysentery when they drank the water, which was brackish and contaminated by their own waste.

The settlers suffered through many difficult times. Conflicts with the Powhatans, the native people already occupying the land when the English arrived, arose regularly. Disputes over land often erupted in battles between the Powhatans and the settlers. Food was always scarce and disease killed off many of the settlers. In 1609–10, the settlement was almost completely wiped out when 400 setters died due to cold, starvation, and disease in what has come to be known as the "starving time."

In 1612 John Rolfe began growing tobacco in Jamestown. After the first shipment of tobacco went to England in 1614, it quickly became the chief export from the New World to England. Jamestown enjoyed a short span of time as a profitable settlement as a result of tobacco exports and then finally was dissolved in the 1620s.

This play should provide your students with many of the basic facts about the Jamestown settlement in a fun and memorable way. The play, a *Jeopardy*-style game show, should serve as a great jumping-off point for you and your students to delve deeper into the inner workings of an early American settlement.

PRODUCING THE PLAY

Because the play covers the entire life span of the Jamestown settlement, you may find reading or performing the play with students most helpful either at the start of your unit as an introductory lesson, or at the end of your unit as a review lesson. Topics touched on here that you may want to explore further include the Virginia Company of London and the business of joint-stock companies in colonial times, England's goals in colonizing the New World, the location of Jamestown and how it was chosen, English relations with the Powhatan, and the "starving time" in the winter of 1609–10.

When reading this play out loud in class, you should note that the roles of Regis History, Dr. Joe, and Fred the Colonist include the largest speaking parts and are best suited for your stronger readers. The other roles are ideal for readers who are not as confident but who can lend their enthusiasm and physical skills to the fun of the play. Feel free to add extra nonspeaking colonists roles in the reenactment sequences for students who would prefer no lines at all. When choosing students to read each role, remember that although the roles of Regis History and Dr. Joe are written as males, they can easily be played by girls. Simply change Dr. Joe to Dr. Joan and Regis to Regina, or let students choose their own character names.

Read-Aloud Plays: Colonial America • Scholastic Teaching Resources

BOOK LINKS

The Corn Raid by James Lincoln Collier (BT Bound, 2001)

Our Strange New Land: Elizabeth's Diary, Jamestown, Virginia, 1609 by Patricia Hermes (Scholastic, 2000)

The Serpent Never Sleeps by Scott O'Dell (Juniper, 1990)

The Jamestown Colony by Gail Sakurai (Children's Press, 1997)

WEB LINKS

The Jamestown Rediscovery: Association for the Preservation of Virginia Antiques. http://www.apva.org/jr.html This site offers a short history of Jamestown, photographs, and map information. Click on "What we have found" to get to the National Geographic Artifacts Gallery, which contains wonderful photos of Jamestown artifacts.

Virtual Jamestown. http://www.iath.virginia. edu/vcdh/jamestown/ This "digital research, teaching and learning project" offers many photographs of maps, documents, and newspapers from the Jamestown settlement.

ACTIVITIES

- **Debate It: Whose Land?** The English settlers had many good reasons for choosing the location of their settlement. However, they didn't understand that the land was already inhabited by the Powhatans. Divide your students into two debate groups: one to represent the English settlers and one to represent the Powhatans. Ask each group to explain why it should have control over the land. When each group has presented its case, have the two groups negotiate a solution that benefits both parties.

- **Timely Travel** Have your students research the route traveled to the New World by the Jamestown settlers on the *Susan Constant,* the *Discovery,* and the *Godspeed.* Provide students with a reproducible world map (or have them use tracing paper over a world map from a textbook). Challenge them to draw the route the ships traveled and use the scale to estimate the distance of the journey. Invite students to use the Internet to find information about the same route via airplane today. How do the travel times compare between a seventeenth-century ship voyage and a twenty-first-century plane ride? Ask students to consider how the length of the ship voyage might have led to unhealthy conditions on the trip. (They might discuss lack of fresh produce and clean water, close living quarters, and lack of medicine.)

- **Charting Successes/Failures** The settlers did many things that made Jamestown a successful colony for a long time. There were also many things that they could have done better. Ask students to name the settlers' successes (such as the harvesting of tobacco) and record their responses on a chart or blackboard. Students can copy the list into their notebooks. Then have them create a T chart below or on a facing page that lists errors the colonists made in the first column (such as settling in such a marshy area) and ways they might have improved on some of their errors in the second.

- **Pocahontas's Story** Read and compare several versions of the story of Pocahontas with your students. This comparison might include the animated movie *Pocahontas.* Ask your students questions such as, Why do you think Pocahontas is remembered? Do you agree with her position toward the colonists? Toward John Smith? Toward her family and tribe? Pair students and have them conduct mock interviews based on the information they've gathered. Each partner can choose a character to play (Pocahontas, Powhatan, the leader, or John Smith, for example). While one student plays her character, the other student acts as the interviewer. Students can record their interviews in writing, on audiotape, or reenact them for the class.

THE FIRST THANKSGIVING

—

The Harvest Feast of 1621

CHARACTERS
(six students)

ROBBIE: *writer and director of play*

MIN: *narrator of play*

EMILY

KARINA

CARLO: *Massasoit in play*

BEN

Read-Aloud Plays: Colonial America • Scholastic Teaching Resources

SETTING: *A classroom in the present day*

A group of students are chatting with each other, making a lot of noise.
Robbie enters and claps his hands loudly to get everyone's attention.

ROBBIE: People! People! Can I have your attention, please?

The group quiets down and stares at Robbie in surprise.

ROBBIE *(Sounding official)*: Thank you for coming here today. As you know, we are here to rehearse our Thanksgiving play for social studies class.

MIN: Um, Robbie, we're here to *write* our Thanksgiving play for social studies class. We can't rehearse something that we haven't even written yet.

ROBBIE: Exactly. And because I am *obviously* the best writer in class, I've written the script. I've also cast all of the parts. I will be the director and . . .

EMILY: Wait a minute! The assignment was to write the play as a group. No one put you in charge.

ROBBIE: I put me in charge.

KARINA: But the rest of us have been doing research all week for this project.

ROBBIE: That's great. If you understand your characters, it will make my job as director much easier. Here are your scripts. *(Robbie passes out the scripts.)* Each one is labeled so you know who you are playing. Min, you're the narrator. Carlo, you get to be the king of the Indians.

CARLO: Do you mean Massasoit?

ROBBIE: Yeah. Sure.

CARLO: He wasn't the "king of the Indians," he was a chief.

BEN: A Native American chief was called a *sachem*—that's what our cast list should say. Since the pilgrims had kings in England, *they* might have called the sachem a king, but really, a sachem wasn't royalty. He was a leader who worked alongside the rest of the tribe.

ROBBIE: Okay, well, Carlo, you get to be Massasoit, the sachem. Now let's get started.

EMILY: Um, Robbie, it says here that . . .

ROBBIE *(Interrupting)*: No more questions. I will take questions at the end of rehearsal. Places, people! *(Min stands while the others sits around the table.)* And . . . action!

Read-Aloud Plays: Colonial America • Scholastic Teaching Resources

MIN (*As the narrator*): In the autumn of 1621, the Pilgrims sat down to eat a great feast with the Wampanoag Indians. Like we do today, the Pilgrims and Indians filled their bellies with turkey, sweet potatoes, corn on the cob, and cranberry sauce.

EMILY: (*As a Pilgrim*): Excuse me, chief . . . ah, Massasoit . . . , could you please pass the ham?

ROBBIE: Hold it! This is all wrong!

MIN: No kidding! This is *all* wrong! They didn't eat ham. There were no pigs in Plymouth in 1621.

ROBBIE: What are you talking about? I meant that Emily's delivery of that line was all wrong. Emily, you have to put some *feeling* into your lines. You have to sound like you *really* want the ham.

EMILY: But Min's right. There were no pigs in Plymouth in 1621, so there was no ham.

BEN: They didn't eat sweet potatoes, either.

KARINA: And the corn they ate wasn't corn on the cob. It was cornmeal made from the Indian corn that the Wampanoag brought to the feast.

ROBBIE: Are you sure about this?

MIN: Positive. And they didn't eat cranberry sauce, either. They didn't have any sugar. You need sugar to make cranberry sauce.

ROBBIE: So what did they do, just munch on plain old cranberries?

BEN: And raspberries and strawberries and grapes and all sorts of other fruits.

ROBBIE: That's ridiculous. Who ever heard of eating grapes at Thanksgiving dinner?

MIN: Maybe no one eats grapes at Thanksgiving dinner now, but in 1621 they most likely did. Did you do any research at all for this play, Robbie, or did you just write a whole script about what you and your family do in November every year?

BEN: The feast we're supposed to be writing about wasn't even in November in 1621. It was in October, after the harvest.

ROBBIE: I know that . . . um . . . The time of my play is October, not November. *Everybody* knows that the first Thanksgiving wasn't in November. I mean, *of course* I know that. Now can we just continue with the play? We have a lot of rehearsing to do, and sitting here yapping isn't getting it done. Places, people! Places! (*Students resume their positions for the rehearsal.*) And . . . action!

Read-Aloud Plays: Colonial America • Scholastic Teaching Resources

CARLO *(as Massasoit)*: Thank you for inviting us to this wonderful dinner. Since you have just arrived aboard the *Mayflower* to be among us, my people and I are pleased about our peace treaty and we are pleased to sit and feast with you on this one night for Thanksgiving dinner.

MIN: Oh, come on, Robbie. How could you get so many things wrong in one little line?

ROBBIE: I was about to ask Carlo the same thing. Carlo, you are Massasoit, the chief Indian. You have to speak like a leader, not a mouse.

CARLO: But the line is all wrong! First of all, the pilgrims had been in Plymouth for nearly a whole year. They arrived in November of 1620, and the feast was in 1621.

BEN: They didn't call it Thanksgiving dinner, either.

KARINA: For the English, it wasn't even a celebration of thanks.

ROBBIE: Of course it was! The Pilgrims were thankful for their peace treaty with the Wampanoag, so they invited them to dinner.

MIN: Well, that's sort of correct. The English and the Wampanoag signed a peace treaty in April of 1621, which made them allies.

EMILY: Right. The Wampanoag wanted the treaty so the English would be their allies when they were arguing with other Native Americans.

BEN: And the English wanted a treaty so they could occupy the land they'd settled without trouble from the Wampanoag.

ROBBIE: Oh, come on! This has nothing to do with Thanksgiving. Let's just get on with the play, okay? Karina, take it from your line, "God, we say our thanks to you on this one Thanksgiving Day for the bountiful feast we have."

KARINA: Robbie, your script has so many mistakes! The English were celebrating a good harvest. Every year they held a *three*-day celebration at the end of their harvest. In 1621, because they had a good relationship with the Wampanoag due to the peace treaty, the English invited them to join their harvest feast.

CARLO: So for the Pilgrims, it wasn't a day of thanking God for anything. When they wanted to thank God they had a day of prayer and fasting. They wouldn't have eaten a giant feast!

ROBBIE: You mean the English were just happy about a good harvest, so they were celebrating?

MIN: Exactly.

ROBBIE (*Sheepishly*): I really *did* make a lot of mistakes in this play.

EMILY: Maybe you shouldn't have written it without the rest of us.

ROBBIE: I guess you're right. You all did a lot more research than I did.

KARINA: I think we should just start over and write the play as a group.

BEN: I second that idea.

MIN: Okay, I've got some paper and a pen in my bag.

Min gets out paper and a pen from her backpack.

CARLO: I think we should make a list of characters first.

EMILY: Well, there was Massasoit, and about 90 other Wampanoag.

MIN: And all of the Pilgrims. I think there were about 50 of them.

ROBBIE: Okay, 50 Pilgrim men.

MIN: What?

ROBBIE: The pilgrims were all men.

MIN: No, they weren't. There were whole families. Men, women, and even children were there.

ROBBIE: Name one woman who was there.

MIN: Elizabeth Hopkins was there with her husband, four kids, and two servants!

EMILY: And Susanna White Winslow was there. She was the first woman to get married in Plymouth. She married Edward Winslow, who was one of the early governors of the colony.

BEN: So we have about 50 English men, women, and children, and about 90 Wampanoag. There aren't enough of us to play all of them.

CARLO: I liked Robbie's idea of having a narrator. We could use a narrator to explain how many people were there.

MIN (*Taking notes*): That's a good idea. Then we wouldn't need 150 actors.

KARINA: Right. Someone could play Massosoit, and someone should play Squanto. He wasn't mentioned in Robbie's play at all.

ROBBIE: Who was Squanto?

KARINA: His real name was Tisquantum, but he is known as Squanto.

Read-Aloud Plays: Colonial America • Scholastic Teaching Resources

EMILY: He was part of the Wampanoag tribes. He was kidnapped by the English when he was very young and taken to Spain to be sold as a slave. He escaped to England where they taught him English and made him an interpreter for Englishmen who were exploring the New World.

MIN: He ended up traveling on the *Mayflower* back to his homeland. He helped his people and the Pilgrims by negotiating the peace treaty between the two.

BEN: We should add him to our cast list. He played an important part in the celebration.

ROBBIE: Wait! Hold everything! Don't add anything yet! I have the best idea! It is way better than my other play. Let's write about the *second* Thanksgiving!

EMILY: What?

ROBBIE: Everyone writes about the first Thanksgiving, which it turns out wasn't even really a Thanksgiving anyway. But you never hear about the second Thanksgiving! I'll bet that in 1622 they had ham and sugar and all the stuff to have a feast like we have today.

KARINA: Except that they didn't have Thanksgiving again until the end of the Revolutionary War.

ROBBIE: Karina, what are you talking about? Why wouldn't they have another harvest feast?

KARINA: Well, small groups might have had other harvest feasts, but there wasn't another big celebration until 1777.

EMILY: And even then it was only a regional holiday. Different groups celebrated at different times.

BEN: But in 1863, when Abraham Lincoln was president, there were two national celebrations of thanks. One was in August after the Union victory at Gettysburg. The other was in November. That was the first official celebration of what we now call Thanksgiving.

ROBBIE: Thanksgiving began during the Civil War?

MIN: Right. Abraham Lincoln thought Americans were very lucky to have a strong harvest and prosper during a civil war. He thought it was something everyone should be thankful for. So he wrote the Thanksgiving Proclamation of 1863, which made the last Thursday in November a national holiday.

ROBBIE: This is incredible. I had no idea that what we always called the first Thanksgiving wasn't really the *first* Thanksgiving at all! The first Thanksgiving, like what we celebrate today, really happened in 1863.

Read-Aloud Plays: Colonial America • Scholastic Teaching Resources

CARLO: So, getting back to our original plan, I think we should stage our autumn harvest play just like it *really* was in 1621.

BEN: I agree. What if we pair off and make lists of important facts that need to be included? Then we can look at the lists and write the play as a *group*. Emily, you and I can work together, and Robbie and Min, and Carlo and Karina.

KARINA: That's a good idea. Carlo, why don't we be in charge of the Pilgrims?

BEN: Then your list should be about the Pilgrims and their religious beliefs and about how and why they came to Plymouth to begin with.

CARLO: Okay.

EMILY: Ben and I can write about the Wampanoag tribe: how their tribe was run and how they lived.

MIN: Robbie, you and I can write about the peace treaty between the Pilgrims and the Wampanoag. I'll help you keep your facts straight!

KARINA: Can I also be in charge of writing about the food at the feast? We can't have an Autumn Harvest play without talking about food.

ROBBIE: Yeah, and we can't have people thinking that the Pilgrims and Wampanoag really ate cornbread and pumpkin pie.

CARLO: Good point . . . . Hey that gives me an idea. Know what I think would be fun? Besides doing the play, why don't we bring in food for the class and have a real feast after the play!

MIN: That *would* be fun!

EMILY: I know how to cook a turkey.

BEN: I'll bring in some wheat flour and cornmeal. I've never just eaten plain cornmeal. I hope it's not too disgusting!

CARLO: Someone should bring some kind of fruit. I guess I could do that.

MIN: Robbie, what are you going to bring? Or will you be too busy directing the rest of us to bring anything?

ROBBIE: Um . . . considering everyone else did so much more work than I did, maybe someone else deserves to be director. I'll bring the fruit, Carlo. I can't wait to go home and tell my parents that we should serve grapes this year at Thanksgiving dinner!

Read-Aloud Plays: Colonial America • Scholastic Teaching Resources

BACKGROUND ON THE FIRST THANKSGIVING

Despite the fact that Thanksgiving is one of America's most important and most celebrated holidays, many misconceptions about its origins persist as popular legend and are even exacerbated with time. This play serves to dispel some of those misconceptions.

In 1620 the group known as the Pilgrims left England to come to America. The Pilgrims were people who left the Church of England in order to practice their own form of religion. Some of these people were known as Separatists, and others, whose mission was to "purify" the English church, were known as Puritans. Collectively they were known as Pilgrims. The Pilgrims first came to the New World in 1620 on *The Mayflower* and later, in 1621 and 1632 on *The Fortune, The Anne,* and *The Little James.*

The *Mayflower* landed on November 22, 1620, in an area of Massachusetts that is now Provincetown, which was already inhabited by a Wampanoag tribe. The Wampanoag was a group of tribes that had resided in that area for thousands of years. Most of the Wampanoag tribes had been wiped out over the years by illness, but one remained, ruled by Massasoit, the sachem, or leader.

Earlier in 1621, with the help of Tisquantum, also known as Squanto, the Pilgrims and the Wampanoag formed a peace treaty together. The peace treaty dictated that no one from either party would harm or bring danger to any member of the other party.

The feast that occurred in 1621, now called "the first Thanksgiving," was actually a fall harvest feast and not a day of giving thanks in the religious sense. The pilgrims had just harvested their first successful crops and were celebrating with a three-day feast. To honor their new relationship with the Wampanoag, the pilgrims invited Massasoit and his tribe to join them. It is this original feast in 1621 that inspired us to celebrate what we now call Thanksgiving—a holiday that we have celebrated nationally since 1863.

PRODUCING THE PLAY

In order to help your students become engaged in this very plain and simple history lesson, this play is written with a student perspective in mind. The students in this play are trying to write a play about the first Thanksgiving for their history class and must deal with some of the issues and frustrations your own students might go through during a group project.

This play can be produced simply by reading it out loud in the classroom or staging it as a short skit. Because the setting is a modern classroom, you need not worry about special costuming or set pieces. The characters are fictional students rather than historical people, so students may more easily relate to the characters and more readily grasp the concepts presented. In fact, you may find it helpful to substitute your students' real names for the character names listed in the script. You should also feel free to change the male characters to female or vice versa as needed. Should you choose to add roles in order to use more students, feel free to divide any of the roles—other than that of Robbie— into two or more characters.

Prior to reading this play, you might activate background knowledge and uncover some misconceptions about the first Thanksgiving by asking students to share how they see the first Thanksgiving taking place and also how they observe Thanksgiving at home today. You may also want to consider asking your students to bring in autumn harvest foods and have a feast after performing the play, just as the students in the play plan to do.

READ-ALOUD PLAYS: COLONIAL AMERICA

WEB LINKS

The Pilgrim Hall Museum: America's Museum of Pilgrim Possessions. http://www.pilgrimhall.org/plgrmhll.htm This site offers extensive information and illustrations of the lives of the pilgrims, from their journeys to the New World to the Mayflower Compact and the First Thanksgiving.

Wampanoag Indians: The Boston Children's Museum. http://www.bostonkids.org/teachers/TC/ Connect with this site to find information about the Wampanoag tribes as well as lesson-planning help, photographs, books, and other resources.

BOOK LINKS

Squanto's Journey: The Story of the First Thanksgiving by Joseph Bruchac (Silver Whistle, 2000)

William Bradford: Rock of Plymouth by Kieran Doherty (Twenty-First Century/Millbrook, 1999)

Giving Thanks: The 1621 Harvest Feast by Kate Waters (Scholastic Press, 2001)

ACTIVITIES

- *Thanksgiving: Past and Present* As the characters in this play point out, the traditional turkey and cranberry sauce and stuffing dinner that we eat in America today was not actually what the Pilgrims and Indians ate in 1621. Ask your students to compare their Thanksgiving meals with the harvest feast described in the play. Discuss reasons why the meal in 1621 did not contain much of what we eat today. For example, why might they not have had pumpkin pie in 1621? Have students research what foods and spices the colonists did have and, as a group, plan a menu for a dinner modeled after the feast of 1621.

- *The First Thanksgiving: Take Two!* The students in this play are supposed to write a short account of the first Thanksgiving. Ask

your students to do the same thing. Divide them into small groups and have each group write a short play based on the first Thanksgiving. They may use some of the ideas generated by the students in the read-aloud play.

- *Illustrated Outfits* The colonists and the Wampanoag wore very different clothing, each influenced by their lifestyles, work, environment, and religious beliefs. Have students research each group and discuss what they wore and why (i.e., many of the colonists were Puritans whose religion dictated simple, conservative clothing). Ask your students to draw a person in traditional clothing from each group, paying careful attention to the clothing and labeling parts of the outfit in the picture to highlight new vocabulary.

- *Why Celebrate? Thanksgiving Proclamations* Read the First Thanksgiving Proclamation of 1676 and the Thanksgiving Proclamation of 1863 out loud in class. How is the tone of the 1676 proclamation different than it might have been had it been written in 1621? How had the colonists' relationships with the local Native American groups changed? Now compare this seventeenth-century proclamation with Lincoln's proclamation. How are they similar? How are they different? What is the new purpose of the Thanksgiving celebration according to Lincoln? Discuss why Thanksgiving was made a national holiday. You can find the First Thanksgiving Proclamation at **http://www.law.ou.edu/hist/thanksgiv.html** and the Thanksgiving Proclamation of 1863 at **http://members.aol.com/calebj/proclamation.html**.

© Read-Aloud Plays: Colonial America • Scholastic Professional Books

A TRIANGLE OF TRADE

—

The Colonial Slave Trade

CHARACTERS

ALEXANDER GRAHAM BELL: *narrator*

CHRISTOPHER COLUMBUS: *explorer for Spain*

RODRIGO: *Columbus's assistant*

QUEEN ISABELLA: *Queen of Spain* • KING MANUEL I: *King of Portugal*

DIOGO: *explorer for Portugal* • ESTEVAO: *Portuguese trader*

KING BABU: *West African king*

JAMES CARVER: *plantation owner* • WILLIAM ATHERTON: *slave trader*

ENSLAVED AFRICAN 1 • ENSLAVED AFRICAN 2

MR. REILLY: *insurance agent* • KING FYNN: *King of Ghana*

KING GEORGE II: *King of England*

JANE: *English citizen* • THOMAS JACKSON: *plantation owner*

JACOB: *African slave*

Read-Aloud Plays: Colonial America • Scholastic Teaching Resources

ALEXANDER GRAHAM BELL *(to the audience)*: Hello. My name is Alexander Graham Bell. You should know right off the bat that I have absolutely nothing to do with the subject matter of this play, which is slave commerce in colonial America, also known as the triangle trade. In fact, I wasn't even born until 1847. In this play I am the narrator and the telephone operator.

Now I didn't actually invent the telephone until the year 1876. The playwright has decided to use the telephone to help tell the story of the triangle trade and how it grew during the colonial period. Although all of the characters use modern ways to communicate, you should keep in mind that, before the phone was invented, it often took many weeks to get a message across the Atlantic Ocean.

Our story begins with a man whose name you might know: Christopher Columbus.

ACT 1

SETTING: *Spain and a Caribbean island, 1492*

Christopher Columbus and Rodrigo enter.

CHRISTOPHER COLUMBUS: We can set up camp right over there, Rodrigo.

Rodrigo's cell phone rings. He looks at the caller ID.

RODRIGO: It's Queen Isabella, sir.

COLUMBUS: What does she want now?

Columbus hits the Talk button.

COLUMBUS: Hello, Your Illustrious Highness.

Queen Isabella enters. She plays with a gold necklace she is wearing.

QUEEN ISABELLA: Oh, oh, oh! Chris, I just love my gorgeous new necklace. Where did you get it?

COLUMBUS: I had it made from the gold we found here.

QUEEN ISABELLA: Oh, that's sweet . . . Did you say gold? There? In the Orient?

COLUMBUS: Actually, it turns out I didn't hit the Orient. I discovered a new world. And it's just crawling with gold. We've been trading food and blankets and other things with some of the natives here for their gold.

QUEEN ISABELLA: Hmmm . . . How interesting.

COLUMBUS: I didn't want to tell you right away, but it seems I'm going to have to try again to find that route to India.

QUEEN ISABELLA: Oh, no, no, no, Chris. You just keep on exploring that new world. We don't need the Orient. You just make sure that the New World belongs to Spain.

COLUMBUS: But, Your Majesty—

QUEEN ISABELLA: Keep up the good work. Say hi to the crew.

COLUMBUS: But—

Queen Isabella hangs up. Columbus exits. Queen Isabella redials the phone. Alexander Graham Bell puts on a headset.

BELL: Long-distance operator.

QUEEN ISABELLA: Get me King Manuel.

BELL: One moment, please. King Manuel of Portugal? There's a call for you from Queen Isabella of Spain.

ACT 2

SETTING: *Spain and Portugal*

King Manuel I enters with a phone in his hand.

KING MANUEL I: Hello, Isabella.

QUEEN ISABELLA: Hi, Manny. Guess what?

KING MANUEL I: I heard, I heard. Columbus found land. I owe you five bucks.

QUEEN ISABELLA: Not only that, he found a whole new world. And it's covered in gold. I'm rich!

KING MANUEL I: Gold? Wow. Good for you. *(Trying to get off the phone)* Oops, I've got to go. Someone's at the door. Toodles.

King Manuel hangs up the phone and quickly redials. Isabella exits.

BELL: Long-distance operator.

KING MANUEL I: King Manuel of Portugal here. I'm trying to reach one of my men who is currently exploring the New World. His name is Diogo. Can you connect me, please?

BELL: One moment, please. Diogo? I have a call from King Manuel of Portugal.

ACT 3

SETTING: *Portugal and what is now Brazil*

Diogo enters with a cell phone in his hand.

DIOGO: Yes.

KING MANUEL I: I just received a call from Queen Isabella. She says there's gold all over the New World.

DIOGO: No gold here, just fields and fields of sugarcane, cotton, tobacco. Forests of trees as far as you can see. There are a lot of other minerals like iron, quartz, and tin here. Not as precious as gold, but very useful in making guns, pots, and pans. There are even acres and acres of coffee beans.

KING MANUEL I: Oh, is that all? Wait a minute! I have an idea. I've got to go.

King Manuel hangs up the phone and quickly redials. Diogo exits.

BELL: Long-distance operator.

KING MANUEL I: Hi. I need to reach one of my men currently exploring in the Orient. His name's Estevao.

BELL: One moment, please . . . Estevao? I have a call from King Manuel of Portugal.

ACT 4

SETTING: *Portugal and the Orient*

Estevao enters with a cell phone in his hand.

ESTEVAO: Yes, go ahead. Hello.

KING MANUEL I: Estevao, I need all men to go to the New World. Portugal is going to get rich!

ESTEVAO: I'm sorry, Your Majesty, but I can't spare any men. We're busy making Portugal rich with all the cloth and spices we're finding here in Asia.

KING MANUEL I: But I need my people to go to the New World right away and work—there's a world of treasures to be mined and harvested there. We're going to ship the metal back to Portugal and make pots, guns, and other goods to sell all over the world.

ESTEVAO: Hold on. I think I have a solution.

Both hang up. King Manuel exits. Estevao redials.

Read-Aloud Plays: Colonial America • Scholastic Teaching Resources

BELL: Long-distance operator.

ESTEVAO: I need to reach King Babu. He's a tribal ruler in western Africa.

BELL: One moment, please. Call for King Babu from Estevao.

ACT 5

SETTING: *The Orient and what is now Nigeria*

King Babu enters with a cell phone in his hand.

KING BABU: Hello.

ESTEVAO: Hi, King Babu. It's Estevao. I remember when we were in Africa you told me how poor your tribe is. Well, I was wondering if you might like some rum, guns, even horses.

KING BABU: Like it? I'd love it! What's the catch?

ESTEVAO: Well, my boss, King Manuel of Portugal, needs some people to work for him in the New World.

KING BABU: I have plenty of people in my kingdom. I'll give you all I can spare.

ESTEVAO: We won't be able to pay them much until we begin making money. But we can use them as indentured servants. We can feed and clothe them in exchange for their work, and they can earn their way out.

KING BABU: Don't worry about paying them. If the goods you send are rich enough, I'll let you take all the workers you need.

Both continue talking quietly into their phones and exit.

BELL: An indentured servant was someone who worked for one particular person, often for very low wages, until he had enough money to buy his freedom. But the greed of the European royalty and African rulers made them strike a deal that would allow the workers to be bought outright and made slaves for life. Now we go to the middle of the seventeenth century, when much of the New World is still being explored, England is the dominant European power active in setting up colonies in North America, and slavery has become part of the colonial economy.

His headset rings.

BELL: Excuse me. I have a call coming in . . . *(Into mouthpiece)* Long-distance operator.

Read-Aloud Plays: Colonial America • Scholastic Teaching Resources

ACT 6

SETTING: *England and what is now Nigeria, the mid-1600s*

James Carver and William Atherton enter with cell phones in their hands.

JAMES CARVER: Please connect me with William Atherton. He's a slave trader in Africa. It's an emergency.

BELL: One moment, please. I have a call from James Carver in England to William Atherton in Africa.

WILLIAM ATHERTON: Please connect us . . . Hello?

CARVER: William, I need more Africans. I'm expanding my plantation over in the colonies, and business is booming.

ATHERTON: I can't give you any more. The boat's full.

CARVER: You have to send more. I'll pay extra.

ATHERTON: Well, when you put it that way . . . I suppose I can squeeze more people in the hold. They might be weak and dirty when they arrive, but I'm sure you can get them right back into shape.

CARVER: Terrific. Thanks, William.

Carver exits.

ACT 7

SETTING: *West Africa*

Atherton pushes Enslaved Africans 1 and 2 toward a ship.

ATHERTON: Hurry up, everybody. We're going to work in the New World. Untold riches will be yours. All aboard!

ENSLAVED AFRICAN 1: But I don't want to leave my home.

ATHERTON: You'll come back soon enough; just like your leaders told you.

ENSLAVED AFRICAN 2: But I'll miss my family. And I'm perfectly happy here in Africa. Just where did you say this New World is?

ATHERTON: That doesn't concern you! *(He cracks a whip and Enslaved African 1 and 2 get scared and start pushing onto the ship.)* Move it! We've got to fit more than five hundred of you onto the ship. There are no seats. Just lie down on the floor and push in!

Enslaved African 1 lies down next to Enslaved African 2
as if he's very cramped.

ENSLAVED AFRICAN 1: Ouch! This is really uncomfortable. What's going to happen to us?

ENSLAVED AFRICAN 2: They mean to put us to work. I hear that many European countries are getting rich and they need more workers. We'll be worked to the bone on farms and plantations.

ENSLAVED AFRICAN 1: I work hard right here at home for myself. And I get to raise my family and live the way I want to.

ENSLAVED AFRICAN 2: I think those days are over.

ENSLAVED AFRICAN 1: Not if I can help it. Look, there are so many of us on this ship. We completely outnumber the crew. I say once we get out on the ocean, we take over the ship and kill these so-called masters.

ENSLAVED AFRICAN 2: That might be our only hope of returning home.

Enslaved Africans 1 and 2 begin whispering their plan
to the others on the ship.

BELL: African captives were bound in chains and forced to live in terrible conditions that caused many of them to die during the Middle Passage, a journey from West Africa to the southern American colonies that often lasted for more than six weeks. Even those who were able to overcome their captors and take over the ships often perished at sea.

ACT 8

SETTING: *Africa and an English colony in what is now Virginia*

Carver enters talking on the phone to Atherton.

CARVER: What happened?

ATHERTON: A mutiny. The slaves rose up and took over the ship. Then it sank in a horrible storm. Everyone was killed.

CARVER: But I have hundreds of plantation owners here at the auction waiting for the latest batch of slaves! I'm not going to be responsible for this!

ATHERTON: I'm sorry, James, but you can't get your money back.

CARVER: I'll fix this.

Carver hangs up and redials. Atherton exits.

Read-Aloud Plays: Colonial America • Scholastic Teaching Resources

BELL: Long-distance operator.

CARVER: Calling England. I would like to speak with Lloyd's of London insurance company, please.

BELL: One moment, please.

ACT 9

SETTING: *The English colony and England*

Mr. Reilly enters and picks up the ringing phone.

MR. REILLY: Lloyd's of London. Mr. Reilly speaking.

CARVER: Hi, Mr. Reilly. I'm a plantation owner and slave trader here in the colony of Virginia. We've been having a terrible time with slave mutinies and slaves dying on the ride over. I was wondering if we might be able to get insurance for that. We'll pay you a fee every month, and if we lose any slaves, you'll pay us for them.

REILLY: Well, we have no such type of insurance policy like that.

CARVER: If you can insure me, I'll tell all the other slave traders about it. They'll sign up for insurance with you as well, and you'll be rich. Then it will really be worth your while to write a policy.

REILLY: Hmmm. That would be quite profitable. You have a deal.

They both hang up and exit.

BELL: The American colonists were able to insure slaves because slavery was legal in England and the colonies.

His headset rings.

BELL: Excuse me. *(Into mouthpiece)* Long-distance operator.

ACT 10

SETTING: *Africa and England, 1772*

King Fynn enters dialing his phone.

KING FYNN: Yes, hello. I'd like to speak to King George the Second of England.

BELL: One moment, please.

King George enters and picks up the ringing phone.

Read-Aloud Plays: Colonial America • Scholastic Teaching Resources

BELL: I have a call to King George the Second of England from King Fynn of Ghana.

KING GEORGE II: His Royal Highness speaking.

KING FYNN: Hi, George. King Fynn here. I noticed you're doing quite well with your American colonies.

KING GEORGE II: Oh, yes. Quite well. Thank you for all you've done.

KING FYNN: That's what I'm calling about. Some of the guns you've sent are misfiring, and this latest batch of rum is awful. You're sending products to me that are less than perfect, and keeping the best for yourself.

KING GEORGE II: I'm sorry. We'll do better. We want every leg of this triangle to work well—getting slaves from Africa to the colonies, raw materials from the colonies to England, and manufactured goods from England back to you in Africa. I want you to be happy.

KING FYNN: I thank you for your understanding, George. I'll tell the rulers of the other African countries how helpful you've been, and I'm sure they'll gladly supply you with slaves as well.

KING GEORGE II: I'm very grateful.

Jane enters already on the phone.

JANE: Ahem!

KING GEORGE II: Oops, hang on. I've got a local call on the other line.

King George presses a button on his phone.

KING GEORGE II: Hello, King George here.

JANE: Hello, King George. I'm an English citizen, and I'm appalled at what's going on in the colonies.

KING GEORGE II: What do you mean? We're doing so well with all of the sugar, cotton, molasses, wood, furs, and such coming from the colonies—

JANE: I am referring to the buying and selling of slaves.

KING GEORGE II: But that really isn't an issue. The slaves aren't from our country. They're Africans.

JANE: They are people nonetheless. And we the people of England want to put a stop to it. This is 1772, after all.

Read-Aloud Plays: Colonial America • Scholastic Teaching Resources

KING GEORGE II: Well, it seems that this is an enlightened age and I must obey the will of the people. I'll take care of it.

King George clicks over. Jane exits.

KING GEORGE II: King Fynn?

KING FYNN: I'm still here.

KING GEORGE II: Um, I have some bad news.

KING FYNN: Uh-oh. What is it?

KING GEORGE II: The people have spoken, and if I don't want a revolution in my country, I have no choice but to abolish the slave trade to the American colonies.

KING FYNN: But that means our African nations will remain poor.

KING GEORGE II: Sorry, Fynn, there's nothing I can do about it. I've got to go; my phone is beeping.

King George clicks over. King Fynn exits.

KING GEORGE II: Hello?

ACT 11

SETTING: *England and Virginia*

Thomas Jackson enters already on the phone.

BELL: I have a call from a Thomas Jackson in Virginia.

KING GEORGE II: Connect us. Yes, Mr. Jackson?

THOMAS JACKSON: What's this I hear about your abolishing slavery, Your Highness?

KING GEORGE II: I didn't abolish slavery. I only abolished the slave trade to the colonies.

JACKSON: But if you abolish the slave trade, how will we get new slaves?

KING GEORGE II: There are thousands of slaves in the colonies now. You have a lot of slaves on your plantation, don't you?

JACKSON: Of course.

KING GEORGE II: Well, as you allow them to have families and their families grow, you'll have plenty of free work hands . . . And then, of course, there are the pirate ships and slave traders from other countries that we British cannot stop.

JACKSON: I didn't think of that.

KING GEORGE II: Mr. Jackson, I understand that slavery is far too profitable to abolish completely. The colonies can continue to have slaves. We just won't get them from Africa and we won't have to supply the African rulers with goods anymore. That part of the triangle is closed.

JACKSON: Okay. I'll spread the news.

He hangs up. King George exits.

JACKSON: Jacob!

Jacob, a slave, enters.

JACOB: Yes, sir.

JACKSON: I want you to take a message to all the plantations in the colony: The triangle trade is over. England has abolished slave trading.

JACOB *(Excited)*: Does that mean I can live as a free man?

JACKSON: No, Jacob. I'm sorry, but slavery is still legal here. We would lose too much money if we allowed you to be free.

JACOB: Can I at least use your phone to call home?

JACKSON: I'm sorry, Jacob. Slaves aren't allowed to use the phone.

Jackson exits. Jacob pauses to sigh and slowly exits.

BELL: As you know, slavery was never abolished in the American colonies. It was finally abolished following the Civil War, long after America had become an independent country.

Read-Aloud Plays: Colonial America • Scholastic Teaching Resources

BACKGROUND OF THE SLAVE TRADE

European colonial powers like England profited from an economic system called mercantilism, which required the people of their colonies to produce and send raw goods back to the mainland. In return, the colonies received manufactured goods produced by the mother country. This policy made the colonial powers rich and ensured the economic dependency of their colonies, which possessed poorer technology and fewer factories. A third trading partner could be added to increase profits for all parties.

This was the case with England, the American colonies, and Africa, who together established a triangular trading partnership from the mid-seventeenth century through the mid-eighteenth century. In their trade agreement, Africa would send slaves to the colonies and the colonies would use the slaves as workers and send the fruits of their labors —raw materials like minerals, sugar, and cotton —to England. England would use these raw materials to manufacture products like pots, fabrics, and guns, and send some of these goods to Africa, which lacked the money and technology to mine its own resources.

The triangular trade arrangement continued until England outlawed slavery in 1772 and halted the slave trade. Unfortunately, the collapse of the triangle trade did not bring about the end of slavery in America. After decades of cheap slave labor, large farms in the southern colonies had become very profitable plantations, producing cotton, tobacco, and other raw goods that were in great demand throughout Europe. The supply of free labor was continued by pirates and non-British slave traders who brought slaves from the West Indies and Africa, and by new generations of slaves raised in the colonies. Slaves were brought up on the plantations and expected to work for the plantation owner for food and shelter for life, without pay, education, or any hope of leaving the plantation.

The Civil War officially ended slavery in the United States, but the ramifications of enslaving a people against their will for profit impact us even today in race relations, issues of corporate responsibility, international trade, and our position on world-wide human rights. This play seeks to provide some economic insights about why European rulers and their colonists agreed to such a morally reprehensible venture and why the African rulers might have joined in despite the harm to their people.

To help your students relate the triangle trade to big business as they already understand it in the fast-moving, real-time world of today's communication, this script employs the convention of the telephone and instant communication. As you introduce the play, you may want to emphasize how slow and difficult overseas communication actually was in the seventeenth century and that, of course, the telephone had not yet been invented.

PRODUCING THE PLAY

If your class is small, you may want to assign each student more than one role since there are 18 characters in this play. For larger classes, several students may share the role of Alexander Graham Bell, the narrator. If you wish to produce this play in your classroom, have students think of simple ways to depict period costumes and locations.

The scene on the slave ship can be portrayed easily by having some students wave a blue cloth on the floor in front of the actors as they are speaking. Aluminum foil and cardboard can create the trappings of the royal characters. Have students think of creative ways to show the changes in location. Could a coat of arms depict the throne room of a European ruler? How about a West African coastal scene behind King Babu or King Fynn to represent where they are? You might record an appropriate tone for each character's phone.

Make sure to invite students to play roles that offer diverse perspectives. Ask them

Read-Aloud Plays: Colonial America • Scholastic Teaching Resources

questions about how they felt playing characters that they might not otherwise be able to relate to. During a first read through, feel free to interrupt the reading to ask students what they think of each of the decisions as it is being made. If your class performs the play for an audience, consider interrupting the action to pose the same questions of the audience.

WEB LINKS

Library of Congress: African American Odyssey. http://memory.loc.gov/ammem/ aaohtml/exhibit/aointro.html A rich, document-based on-line exhibit that traces the roots of the African-American quest for equality, beginning with the history of the slave trade.

The Virginia Foundation for the Humanities and The Digital Media Lab at the University of Virginia Library: The Atlantic Slave Trade and Slave Life in the Americas—A Visual Record http://gropius. lib.Virginia.edu/Slavery/ Dozens of images from maps to illustrations that illustrate all aspects of slavery, from life in precolonial West Africa to religious life on a plantation.

BOOK LINKS

From Slave Ship to Freedom Road by Julius Lester (Dial, 1988)

In the Time of the Drums by Kim L. Siegelson (Jump at the Sun/Hyperion, 1999)

Growing Up in Slavery by Sylvaine A. Diouf (Millbrook Press, 2001)

ACTIVITIES

• *Mapping It Out: Triangular Trade* Break up the class into groups and have each group draw a map of the triangle trade among England, Africa, and the American colonies. Encourage students to use map symbols to show the traded products and write a brief explanation for each leg of the trade triangle on the map.

• *Pen a Proclamation for Freedom* Abraham Lincoln wrote a proclamation to abolish slavery in 1863. Read selections of the Emancipation Proclamation in class and discuss its importance. Have students discuss why people disagreed about whether slavery was good or bad, and ask them to write a short proclamation that would put an end to a kind of oppression that exists in the world today. What might be some arguments against such a document? Find copies of the original manuscript and a transcript on the National Records & Archives Administration Web site at **www.archives.gov/exhibit_hall/ featured_documents/emancipation_ proclamation/index.html**.

• *A Time Line of African-American Achievement* The triangle trade ended in 1772, when England decided to cut direct ties with slavery. Have students discuss why plantation owners continued to use slave labor in the American colonies until the end of the Civil War and how that legacy affects our lives today. Then, make sure to focus on how our culture has been enriched by African Americans. What contributions have African Americans made to science? Education? Entertainment? Students might create a time line of African-American contributions to American history.

• *How Quickly Can You Spread the News?* This play uses Alexander Graham Bell as the narrator and telephone as the main communication device. Of course, the telephone was not invented until 1876—much later than the events of this play. Encourage older students to research methods of communication people used prior to 1876. How did people in Europe communicate with African kings and colonists in the New World? Students might use a T chart to gather information about the differences of communication across distances in 1492 as compared to our modern world of instant communication via cell phones, faxes, E-mail, and so on.

WHAT HAPPENED HERE?

—

The Salem Witch Trials

CHARACTERS

STEPHEN: *a modern-day student*

GOVERNOR PHIPPS: *governor of Massachusetts Colony*

DR. GRIGGS: *physician of Salem*

DEACON NATHANIEL INGERSOLL: *religious leader of Salem*

PHILLIP ENGLISH: *citizen of Salem*

MARY ENGLISH: *citizen of Salem*

JUSTICE SAMUEL SEWELL: *judge from Salem*

NEHEMIAH ABBOT: *citizen of Salem*

THOMAS PUTNAM: *citizen of Salem*

ANN PUTNAM: *daughter of Thomas Putnam*

Read-Aloud Plays: Colonial America • Scholastic Teaching Resources

ACT 1

SETTING: *Study of Governor Phipps, Boston, Massachusetts, 1693*

Stephen, a modern-day student holding a pen and notebook, enters. He looks around a moment before spotting the governor.

STEPHEN: Excuse me, Governor Phipps?

GOVERNOR PHIPPS: Yes, young man?

STEPHEN: My name's Stephen. I'm supposed to do a school report about the Salem witch trials, but so far none of what I've learned makes any sense to me. Since you were the head of the whole Massachusetts Colony, I was hoping you could help me.

GOVERNOR PHIPPS: Sure. What would you like to know?

STEPHEN: What happened here?

GOVERNOR PHIPPS: Your schoolbooks should make it clear, Stephen. Didn't you do your homework?

STEPHEN: Well . . . we read about the trials in school, but it all seems so complicated.

GOVERNOR PHIPPS: Okay, here's what you should know. Between January and October of 1692, nineteen people in Salem Village and nearby areas were found guilty of practicing witchcraft. They were all hanged. Another man was crushed to death. Five others, sadly, died in jail waiting for their trials.

STEPHEN: So in all, twenty-five people died.

GOVERNOR PHIPPS: That's correct, Stephen.

STEPHEN: One was really crushed to death?

GOVERNOR PHIPPS: Yes. Giles Corey. He refused to have a trial.

STEPHEN: So you *crushed* him to death?

GOVERNOR PHIPPS: With boulders. We had to because he refused to have a trial.

STEPHEN: Is that what you usually do when someone refuses a trial? Is that what the law says?

GOVERNOR PHIPPS: Not exactly. We're not in England anymore, you see, and we've had to make our own laws to fit each situation. And these were very unusual cases. We were dealing with witches! We had to do anything we could to solve the problem.

STEPHEN: The problem of witches?

GOVERNOR PHIPPS: Wouldn't you say that having witches in your village was a problem? We had to get rid of them, no matter what! So we held trials.

STEPHEN: How do you hold a trial against someone accused of being a witch?

GOVERNOR PHIPPS: Well, you bring the witch into a room with several judges and question her. Her accusers state the evidence against her, and then the witch must defend herself.

STEPHEN: So they were assumed guilty and found guilty?

GOVERNOR PHIPPS: Yes.

STEPHEN: What kind of evidence did you have against them? Did they turn people into frogs right there in the courtroom or something?

GOVERNOR PHIPPS: Well, no, of course not. Don't be ridiculous!

STEPHEN: Then how did you prove they were witches?

GOVERNOR PHIPPS: There were lots of ways. For example, a number of people said they saw demons flying around the courtroom.

STEPHEN: Did everyone see them?

GOVERNOR PHIPPS: Not everyone . . . that was a problem.

STEPHEN: So you couldn't prove there were demons in the courtroom, and people were convicted without any real proof. How is that fair?

GOVERNOR PHIPPS: You know, Stephen, after the trials in Salem I received a letter from a good citizen named Thomas Brattle about just that. It made me think. So I dissolved the local court, where the first trials were held. I created a superior court where the rest of the trials took place. No evidence of that kind was allowed and no one else was convicted. We do try to do things the right way here in the colony of Massachusetts.

STEPHEN: It still sounds crazy to me!

GOVERNOR PHIPPS: Maybe you should go to Salem Village and speak to Dr. William Griggs. His diagnosis started the whole thing.

STEPHEN: I will. Thank you for your help, Governor.

Read-Aloud Plays: Colonial America • Scholastic Teaching Resources

ACT 2

SETTING: *Home of Dr. Griggs in Salem*

Stephen enters and approaches Dr. Griggs.

STEPHEN: Dr. Griggs, I'm studying the Salem witch trials, and I want to ask you what happened here?

DR. GRIGGS: Elizabeth Parris and Abigail Williams were behaving strangely, so I examined them.

STEPHEN: Who were they?

DR. GRIGGS: Two girls from Salem Village.

STEPHEN: So you examined them. What did you find?

DR. GRIGGS: It was very simple: The girls were bewitched. Several others were, too. Soon the entire colony could have come under the spell of witches.

STEPHEN: How do you know when someone is bewitched?

DR. GRIGGS: Well, the symptoms are . . . very . . . strange.

STEPHEN: Would you please try to explain them?

DR. GRIGGS: The girls were screaming out like they were being hit and pushed, yet no one was touching them. Their bodies would move like that as well. They were seeing all manner of spirits.

STEPHEN: Could you see these spirits?

DR. GRIGGS: Don't be silly, Stephen. I wasn't the one who was bewitched. Only the girls could see them. They also had "witchmarks" on their bodies.

STEPHEN: What are "witchmarks"?

DR. GRIGGS: Bruises on their bodies.

STEPHEN: *(He rolls up the leg of his pants.)* Like this?

DR. GRIGGS: Yes!

STEPHEN: I tripped and fell.

DR. GRIGGS: Are you sure?

STEPHEN: Yes! Dr. Griggs, the point is, couldn't the girls have been making the "witchmarks" themselves? Maybe they fell down or bumped into something.

DR. GRIGGS: Stephen, I am an educated man and a doctor. I would know if they were making it up, or if they bumped into something, as you say. At first some of the marks made me think it was another outbreak of smallpox. And then I thought those girls were merely hysterical. But other young girls soon came forward to say they had been bewitched, too. Since I could find nothing physically wrong with them, it had to be witchcraft.

STEPHEN: Couldn't you help them?

DR. GRIGGS: I'm a doctor. It's clergy's job to cast out evil. I only deal with medical problems.

STEPHEN: What happened to the girls?

DR. GRIGGS: They were taken to the Salem Town magistrates, John Hawthorne and Jonathan Corwin.

STEPHEN: What happened then?

DR. GRIGGS: You'll have to go talk to the magistrates about that. I wasn't there. Better yet, go talk to the Deacon Nathaniel Ingersoll. They all met at his house.

STEPHEN: This isn't getting any clearer!

ACT 3

SETTING: *Home of Nathaniel Ingersoll in Salem Village*

Stephen enters and approaches Deacon Ingersoll.

STEPHEN: Deacon Ingersoll, I've just spoken with Dr. Griggs about the witchcraft trials in Salem. It still doesn't make sense. Can you tell me what happened here?

NATHANIEL INGERSOLL: We are a God-fearing people here in Salem. We believe in good and evil, and Stephen, when evil came, we took action.

STEPHEN: What action did you take?

NATHANIEL INGERSOLL: Those girls were possessed. We asked them to say who possessed them.

STEPHEN: And what did they say?

NATHANIEL INGERSOLL: They said that Sarah Good, Sarah Osborne, and Tituba, Reverend Parris's slave, had put them under a spell.

Read-Aloud Plays: Colonial America • Scholastic Teaching Resources

THE SALEM WITCH TRIALS

STEPHEN: I read in a book that Tituba admitted to practicing voodoo and possessing those girls.

NATHANIEL INGERSOLL: She did admit it, but not at first. We had to beat her.

STEPHEN: You beat a confession out of her?

NATHANIEL INGERSOLL: Stephen, when evil is hiding, you've got to flush it out, no matter what methods you use. I think there are still witches on the loose. As a matter of fact, you should talk to Phillip and Mary English. They ran away when Philip was accused. I'm sure he has something to hide. But I hear he's in New York now.

STEPHEN: Thank you for your help, Deacon Ingersoll.

NATHANIEL INGERSOLL: I hope you learn something useful.

ACT 4

SETTING: *Home of Phillip and Mary English in New York*

*Stephen sits in the kitchen. Mary English brings him a cup of tea
and then sits next to her husband.*

STEPHEN: Mr. and Mrs. English, I want to ask you a few questions about the trials in Salem.

PHILLIP ENGLISH: Those people of Salem—

MARY ENGLISH: They hated everyone who wasn't one of them.

STEPHEN: What do you mean "one of them"?

MARY ENGLISH: An insider, as it were. I married a Frenchman, and they didn't like that.

PHILLIP ENGLISH: They didn't like that I was French. They didn't like that I had money.

STEPHEN: Why didn't they like the French? They just didn't like outsiders?

MARY ENGLISH: Right. And they certainly didn't like that we were making friends with some of the powerful people in Massachusetts.

PHILLIP ENGLISH: And I am an Anglican.

STEPHEN: A what?

PHILLIP ENGLISH: An Anglican. That's my religion. I am not a Puritan, and to them, that was the last straw.

Read-Aloud Plays: Colonial America • Scholastic Teaching Resources

STEPHEN: You think you were accused because you weren't a Puritan?

PHILLIP ENGLISH: I think we were accused because we weren't the same as everyone else.

MARY ENGLISH: I was a woman willing to say what I thought. I was willing to say that what the trials were doing to our beautiful town was wrong.

PHILLIP ENGLISH: They ruined lives. They ruined *our* lives. Look around you, Stephen. Once we had everything. Now we have nothing. We had to move away from Salem. They took all the property I had.

MARY ENGLISH: When someone was accused, they took everything that person owned. And whether you were found guilty or innocent, they used it to pay the court costs. Now we don't have anything.

STEPHEN: Wow. I'm sorry. I never knew all of this. Would you mind if I stayed here for the night? In the morning, I'll go back to Salem to talk with Justice Sewell, the judge from the trials.

MARY ENGLISH: Do you think we'll be able to get our property back?

STEPHEN: I'm only a kid with a history paper to write. But I did read that some of the innocent people got some of their money back.

MARY ENGLISH: Whatever you can do, Stephen, we would appreciate. And of course you are welcome to stay here.

ACT 5

SETTING: *Home of Samuel Sewell in Salem*

Stephen enters and approaches Samuel Sewell.

STEPHEN: Justice Sewell, I'm Stephen, and I—

SAMUEL SEWELL: I know who you are, Stephen, and I knew you would be coming. You are here to ask about the trials in Salem.

STEPHEN: Yes.

SAMUEL SEWELL: I was wrong.

STEPHEN: Excuse me?

SAMUEL SEWELL: We were wrong.

STEPHEN: I'm sorry . . . ?

Read-Aloud Plays: Colonial America • Scholastic Teaching Resources

SAMUEL SEWELL: We did the wrong thing. We believed the accusations and held trials based on our beliefs instead of the facts. We thought we were doing the work of God. And in that sense, we did the best we could.

STEPHEN: Do you regret what happened?

SAMUEL SEWELL: That some people died? That we condemned them to be hanged? No, sir. I said that we conducted the trials poorly. But for all we know, Stephen, those folks were, in fact, witches. And in that sense, we did the right thing.

STEPHEN: Why were most of the accused women, or a different race, like the slave Tituba? Or a different religion, like the Englishes, who were Anglican and not Puritan?

SAMUEL SEWELL: Stephen, you are not a Puritan.

STEPHEN: No, sir.

SAMUEL SEWELL: Then you may not understand the challenges we face. Our Puritan forefathers left England to find a place where they could worship in the way they chose. One of the reasons they were forced to leave England was because of our belief that we are God's chosen people. We must be wary of people who are different from us—

STEPHEN: But those people weren't hurting anyone.

SAMUEL SEWELL: Ah, but many of them did own property or had money, and they refused to give to the church. Even if they were not witches, don't you think they were doing wrong?

STEPHEN: It's not my place to judge.

SAMUEL SEWELL: But it was mine. And as I said, we went about it the wrong way, but we did the best we could.

STEPHEN: What about the innocent people who died?

SAMUEL SEWELL: We did the best we could.

STEPHEN: Were any of the accused found innocent?

SAMUEL SEWELL: If we knew they were innocent, we let them go. Talk to Nehemiah Abbot. He was accused, but we found him innocent. He's just fine now.

Read-Aloud Plays: Colonial America • Scholastic Teaching Resources

ACT 6

SETTING: *Home of Nehemiah Abbot in Salem*

Stephen enters and approaches Nehemiah Abbot, an elderly man.

STEPHEN: Mr. Abbot, my name is Stephen. I've been talking to people around here about the witch trials and I'm told that you were accused. Can you tell me what happened here?

NEHEMIAH ABBOT: I have nothing to say. I'm a free man and I just want to be left alone.

STEPHEN: You were accused by Mary Walcott?

NEHEMIAH ABBOT: I really would like to get back to my weaving, if you please.

STEPHEN: But I have to know: Why do you think you went free?

NEHEMIAH ABBOT: Why? Because I wouldn't stand for it, that's why!

STEPHEN: What did you do differently from the others?

NEHEMIAH ABBOT: Look, that wasn't the first time people were accused of being witches, and in Massachusetts it probably won't be the last. Puritans are scared, superstitious people.

STEPHEN: Why did they let *you* go?

NEHEMIAH ABBOT: Mary Walcott was seventeen years old. She was older than the other accusers, Abigail Williams and Betty Parris and the rest, but still a child. She said I came to her as a specter. A ghost. Now, I'd like to think that I would know if I had come to anybody, even as an apparition, which, of course, I didn't.

STEPHEN: I see.

NEHEMIAH ABBOT: The magistrates said to me that my case was "all but proven" and that I should ask for the "mercy of God." That's when I looked right at Mary Walcott and said, "I speak before God that I am clear from this accusation in all respects."

STEPHEN: But a lot of people denied the charges of witchcraft.

NEHEMIAH ABBOT: Yes, and they also jumped up and down and yelled and pleaded for their lives. That was more reason for the judges to believe they were possessed. Plus, every time someone got excited about the trial, those little girls

Read-Aloud Plays: Colonial America • Scholastic Teaching Resources

THE SALEM WITCH TRIALS

would start cackling and flapping their arms and saying that the accused person was making them do it. Not many people were brave enough to look right at their accusers and say, "I am not a witch."

STEPHEN: What happened next?

NEHEMIAH ABBOT: They took me out of the courtroom so they could look at my face in the bright sunlight. When Mary Walcott came close to me I looked her straight in the eye. Then she said the specter looked like me, but it wasn't me. They let me go.

STEPHEN: Were you surprised when they let you go?

NEHEMIAH ABBOT: Even when Mary Walcott said it wasn't me, Ann Putnam insisted it was. The magistrates had one person's word against another's. It could have gone either way.

STEPHEN: I don't understand why Ann Putnam continued to accuse you.

NEHEMIAH ABBOT: She used her voice, but her father chose the names.

STEPHEN: What?

NEHEMIAH ABBOT: Her father, Thomas Putnam—an important citizen of Salem and also a prominent member of the church. He told her whom to accuse. You should go and see him.

STEPHEN: I will, sir. I'm sorry to have bothered you.

NEHEMIAH ABBOT: After the trials, it's going to take a lot more than you to bother me.

ACT 7

SETTING: *Home of Thomas Putnam in Salem*

*Stephen enters and approaches Thomas Putnam and his twelve-
year-old daughter, Ann.*

STEPHEN: Mr. Putnam, I'm learning about the Salem witch trials and I've heard you played a big part. Can you tell me what happened here?

THOMAS PUTNAM: You know what happened here. Evil was stopped. Witches were put to death. There would have been many more if Governor Phipps had not moved the trial to the superior court and changed the rules, and if good people had not become scared to come forward with more accusations.

Read-Aloud Plays: Colonial America • Scholastic Teaching Resources

STEPHEN: I understand that Ann was one of the chief accusers. I'd like to talk to her.

THOMAS PUTNAM: I'm sure you know everything she had to say. Some in Salem were against my wife and me. Some were against Reverend Parris, and he was a fine man—our spiritual leader and one of the first to try to put a stop to this abomination. A fine man.

STEPHEN: But I don't think the people you call witches did anything wrong. They didn't hurt anyone.

THOMAS PUTNAM: Saying that these witches did not afflict my daughter is like saying that my wife is not a fine woman, or that Reverend Parris is not a fine man . . . *(He turns to Ann.)* Ann?

ANN PUTNAM: I was afflicted by witches.

STEPHEN: Well, it's very hard to argue with that.

THOMAS PUTNAM: You don't understand how things were here in Salem. We didn't want this trouble, or trials, or hangings. But some people wanted all the money, or land, or God for themselves. And the fine people of Salem can't have that. It's not the Puritan way. Do you understand that?

STEPHEN: I think I'm beginning to, a little, maybe . . . You accused people who had too much land or money, right? You were worried that they would steal from you?

THOMAS PUTNAM: I think we are done here.

STEPHEN: If you don't mind, I'd like to make some notes for my report before I go.

THOMAS PUTNAM: Fine. Show yourself out when you're done. Come with me, Ann.

Thomas and Ann Putnam exit. Stephen writes in his notebook.

STEPHEN: I think I get it now. It looks like, for a period of time, the entire village of Salem went kind of insane. It seems like a big plot to keep the wealth of a few safe against what they thought was some sort of threat from outsiders— and to make an example of those who were not Puritans. The powerful people encouraged these young girls to make accusations, and the rest of the village thought that there was something evil in their midst. In the end, it seems, many innocent people died because of simple fear and greed.

Ann Putnam enters the room.

ANN PUTNAM: Stephen?

STEPHEN: Ann.

Read-Aloud Plays: Colonial America • Scholastic Teaching Resources

ANN PUTNAM: I just wanted to say I'm sorry.

STEPHEN: For what?

ANN PUTNAM: For all the trouble. For the people who died. I don't like what happened.

STEPHEN: You're just a kid, like me. I don't think it was your fault.

ANN PUTNAM: I keep thinking of that little girl.

STEPHEN: What little girl?

Ann Putnam begins crying.

ANN PUTNAM: Dorcas Good. She was only four years old, and we said she was a witch.

STEPHEN: Was she hanged with the others?

ANN PUTNAM: No, but she was chained up in the jail. And she just cried and cried for her mother. She won't ever be right in the head again, they said. They said she went insane.

STEPHEN: It wasn't your fault.

ANN PUTNAM: I don't think there were any witches.

STEPHEN: I think maybe you're right.

ANN PUTNAM: I'm sorry.

Stephen smiles.

STEPHEN: I'll make sure people understand what really happened here.

ANN PUTNAM: Thank you, Stephen.

Ann Putnam smiles and runs from the room.

Read-Aloud Plays: Colonial America • Scholastic Teaching Resources

BACKGROUND OF
THE SALEM WITCH TRIALS

In 1692, a number of citizens in the village of Salem, Massachusetts, were accused of witchcraft and put on trial. The reasons for these accusations ranged from land ownership squabbles to differences in religious beliefs, all under the guise of a quest to destroy "evil" in the colony. The Salem witch hunts proved deadly; twenty-five accused "witches" were put to death or died in jail within a period of several months, before widespread hysteria forced the governor to intercede and put an end to the local trials. (Note: You may want to dispel the common myth that those accused of being witches in Salem were burned at the stake. All who were found guilty were hanged except for Giles Corey, who was crushed to death by weight of a large stone.)

A key to making sense of the witch trials is to understand the Puritan mind-set and how religion influenced everyday life in seventeenth-century New England. The church provided a strict moral code and administered justice according to the Scriptures. Anything that was deemed by the church to be an infraction against the Bible was dealt with harshly. For example, swearing, lying, or working or playing on the Sabbath might result in a trip to the stocks or even jail time.

In this church-run society, many of those accused of witchcraft faced a court that would be unrecognizable to Americans today. The village court, headed by a panel of religious leaders rather than secular judges, allowed circumstantial evidence to be brought against the accused and administered justice arbitrarily. Our current legal system, which honors a fair trial and assumes the accused is innocent until proven guilty, wasn't set in place until these codes were laid out in the Constitution in 1787.

To understand more fully about the Salem witch trials, this play focuses on root causes, such as gender relations in a patriarchal society, the strong role of the church in colonial governments, the government's part in defining a moral code, and xenophobia (fear of foreigners or outsiders). This will allow you to open up classroom discussion to important issues that still affect us today.

PRODUCING THE PLAY

The character of Stephen serves as a guide through this distressing period of colonial American history. Like the students in your class, Stephen is trying to learn about and understand the Salem witch trials. As he interviews people who were involved in the trials, he experiences some of the confusion that your students may experience as they learn about this event.

You may want to cast several students in the role of Stephen since it is the one part that continues through the entire play. Also note that Stephen can become Stephanie so that a girl can play the part.

Since there are many different scenes in the play that require Stephen to travel from one location to another, you may want to use music to denote these changes. A student who plays an instrument can play a simple tune that suggests traveling. You might also use a CD or audiotape to set the tone and signal cues.

WEB LINKS

Discovery School: Salem Witch Trials. www.school.discovery.com/schooladventures /salemwitchtrials/index.html A set of great teacher and student reference pages on life in 1692 Salem, historical figures involved, and more.

Salem Witch Trials Documentary Archive and Transcription Project. http:// Jefferson.village.Virginia.edu/salem/home.html Includes primary-source documents around

1692 Salem and the witch trials. NOTE: Please preview the documents carefully before presenting them to students; some of the testimonials can be quite graphic in language and content.

BOOK LINKS

Tituba of Salem Village by Ann Petry (HarperCollins, 1991)

The Witchcraft of Salem Village by Shirley Jackson (Random House, 1999)

The Salem Witch Trials, ed. Laura Marvel (Greenhaven Press, 2002).

A Break with Charity: A Story about the Salem Witch Trials by Ann Rinaldi (Harcourt, 1994) (fiction)

ACTIVITIES

• ***Three Points of View*** Divide your class into three groups and have each group write from the viewpoint of one of the three following characters: Ann Putnam, Dr. Griggs, or Governor Phipps. Ask the group assigned to Ann Putnam to write a speech to apologize and explain the reasons behind her accusations. Have the group representing Dr. Griggs write his testimony during the trials. What evidence might he give in order to accuse the "witches"? Tell the group representing Governor Phipps to write an argument stating why he thinks he acted fairly during the trials. Let each group read its work out loud and then discuss.

• ***Class Query: Salem Trials*** Ask students to put themselves in Stephen's place. Discuss his method of getting the information he needed in order to write his paper. Brainstorm with students other questions that Stephen could have asked the citizens of Salem in order to better understand what happened there. Post a large sheet of paper on the wall and create a K-W-L chart, letting students fill in the information they've learned in the K (Know) section, and the questions they've

generated in the W (Want to know) section. Keep the chart posted. As your unit on this topic continues, invite students to fill in the L (what I've Learned) section with answers to their questions.

• ***The Salem Trials and the Constitution*** Many amendments to the Constitution are meant to prevent events like the Salem witch trials from happening again. The trials took place long before the Constitution of the United States was written. Have your students review the amendments of the Constitution and discuss which amendments would have directly affected the way the trials were carried out. For example, the Fifth Amendment states that no person can be "deprived of life, liberty, or property, without due process of law." Discuss this idea of "due process" and how it would have prevented the trials from unfolding as they did.

For information about the Constitution, go to **http://www.house.gov/Constitution/Amend.html**.

• ***Could It Happen Today?*** Discuss the legal system used in Salem during the time of the witch trials and how it differs from our current legal system. Pose the following questions to students: Do you think that what happened in Salem could happen today? Why or why not? Students can write an outline of an argument for an oral presentation or write a full persuasive essay that explains their reasons.

FOUR HOMES

—

Different Perspectives: French, Spanish, English
(New England and Southern Slaveholding) Colonies

CHARACTERS

SARAH: *an English colonist from Virginia*

BRIEN: *a French trapper from Canada*

MARCEL: *a Yuma Indian from the Mission of San Diego*

HANNAH: *an escaped African slave from Virginia*

All characters are around twelve years old.

SETTING: *A thick and quiet forest somewhere in the northern part of Virginia Colony around 1767*

Brien and Marcel sit around a small fire in a clearing and share a laugh. Sarah breaks through the brush into the clearing, sees the boys, and screams. Brien and Marcel scream and jump up quickly.

SARAH: Who are you?

BRIEN: Who are we? Who are *you*?

MARCEL: Yes, who are you?

SARAH: I'm Sarah.

MARCEL: What are you doing here?

SARAH: What are *you* doing here?

BRIEN: She's English. She's up to no good.

SARAH: What does that mean?

BRIEN: Spying on the French. You're looking for French land to capture and call your own, aren't you?

SARAH: I am not a spy! Why would I be? My father says that the French and English are at peace since the Seven Years' War.

MARCEL: Then what are you doing here?

SARAH: I'm—

*Hannah comes through the brush. Brien and Marcel scream.
Sarah screams at their screams.*

HANNAH: What?

SARAH: Stop screaming! It's Hannah.

BRIEN: Another spy!

SARAH: Hannah is not a spy. She's a slave. I'm helping her run away.

BRIEN: A runaway?

MARCEL: A runaway! Like me. I'm a runaway.

HANNAH: Who are you running away from?

MARCEL: I'm running from the Spanish missionaries. I'm from San Diego.

SARAH: Where's that?

MARCEL: West of here, on the Pacific Ocean. It's so far west that even the trees look very different than they do here. I wanted to get away from the mission where I lived. Many of my people were planning to rebel against the Spanish padres, and my parents wanted me to get as far away from there in case the Spanish tried to kill us. I traveled with traders who were heading east for a long time.

BRIEN: His name is Marcel. I'm Brien. I'm French. We're part of the Métis people.

They all greet each other and sit down.

SARAH: What is the Métis?

BRIEN: My folks came from France. We came to the New World to make our fortune from trapping and exploring new land. We made allies of many Indian tribes.

SARAH: Are you running away, too?

BRIEN: Why do you want to know?

SARAH: I am not a spy!

BRIEN: Maybe not. No, I'm not running away. I was trapping with my father and I got lost. I was traveling alone for a long time before I came across Marcel.

SARAH: You were trapping?

BRIEN: Yes. My father and I set traps in the woods. We trap animals for their skin and fur, their pelts. We also hunt animals like buffalo and elk for leather and food. I hunted for the buffalo that makes up the fur and buckskin in my clothes. My mother sewed it together for me.

Brien stands to show his clothing. Marcel stands to compare clothes.

MARCEL: My clothes are leather, too. Except mine are made for hotter weather and don't have any fur on them. Yours seem like they're made to keep you warm in a cold winter.

BRIEN: They are sort of similar. The design is like the French styles that my parents knew in Europe, but it's combined with the Indian styles they learned here.

MARCEL: That must be why they're so similar. I'm an Indian.

SARAH: Really? What tribe?

MARCEL: We were called Yuma.

SARAH: What do you mean "were"?

MARCEL: When the Spanish missionaries came, they made us renounce our culture. They didn't let us speak our own language or worship the way we used to. That was in the time of my grandfather. Now my whole tribe lives in their mission. The padres—the monks—teach us Spanish and how to pray to their God.

HANNAH: Your padres might not let you speak or pray the way you want to, but at least they let you learn. We can't study anything. It's against the law to teach slaves to read and write.

SARAH: I think that's awful. I love school. We go to the schoolhouse in our village and read from hornbooks and write. I just got my first quill and hornbook. I brought them along so I could teach Hannah to read.

Sarah pulls an example of a hornbook from her satchel and passes it around to the others.

HANNAH: I've just learned the alphabet and I already love reading. You must be right about school, Sarah. Reading sure beats working from sunup to sundown in the fields picking cotton.

BRIEN: Was that your job?

HANNAH: Yes, I was with the picking crew. I didn't have the hardest job—baling the cotton. Mostly the men and boys do that. But being out under the sun in the fields is hot and tiring. The worst job is picking the seeds out of the cotton bolls it so it can be turned into thread for fabric. *(Hannah pulls a cotton boll from her pocket and holds it in her hand.)* I keep one in my pocket to remind me of what I'm running away from.

MARCEL: How do you do that—the picking?

HANNAH: Here, I'll show you. *(Hannah demonstrates picking the little green seeds out.)* You see, the little green seeds are kind of sticky, so you need to make sure to get all of them. It makes your hands hurt after a while, and there's always so much cotton to do this to.

Hannah lets the others look at the cotton boll and then puts it away.

BRIEN: Do you ever get a break?

HANNAH: Sunday is our only day off.

Read-Aloud Plays: Colonial America • Scholastic Teaching Resources

SARAH: That sounds so rough. Our village in Virginia is small, but almost everyone there has a farm. I have to help on the farm, especially around harvest time. The rest of the year I make soap and candles and help my mother sew all the clothes.

MARCEL: Candle making was a big job on the mission, too, but it was a special job, along with making things from metal. Mostly, I gathered olives or chased birds from the fields. Other than making the adobe bricks for the mission, that's pretty much all the Spanish allow us to do. They get to be the padres or soldiers.

SARAH: Oh, I feel so terrible.

BRIEN: How come?

SARAH: Your lives sound so hard. So much of it is work and hardships. We work hard, but we also have a lot of time to do things we love.

BRIEN: Like what?

SARAH: Well, we play games and have toys. My friends and I play games like tag, leapfrog, hopscotch, and checkers, which we play with little wooden pieces. I have a lot of dolls that my mother made for me out of extra material and wooden horses that my father made for me. My brothers and their friends play a game called rounders. They hit a small ball with a stick. It's even fun to watch.

BRIEN: You shouldn't feel bad. I might not have all that you have, but we play games and build toys, too. We also spend a lot of nights singing and dancing. Our dancing is fast and energetic like fire flames, and it can be as tiring as working all day.

Brien laughs at the thought of it.

MARCEL: It's the same for us. One of the Yuma traditions that we still practice is the way we sing and dance. We also play *pokean*. It's a game where you try to hit a cornhusk stuck with feathers into the air using a board attached to a stick. I showed Brien how to play earlier.

Marcel takes out of his pack a battledore, which resembles a Ping-Pong paddle made with a stick tied to a board, and a shuttlecock, which is a homemade version of the one used in badminton, and hands them to Hannah.

BRIEN: Try it, Hannah. We had fun seeing who could hit it in the air the highest or who could keep it up in the air the longest by hitting it over and over again.

Hannah tries to play, hitting the shuttlecock up in the air with the stick a few times until she realizes how hard it is to master. Then she sits and hands the game back to Marcel.

Read-Aloud Plays: Colonial America • Scholastic Teaching Resources

SARAH: That looks like fun.

HANNAH: It is, but it's hard to do. We used to make up games using whatever we had on hand, like wood, scraps of material, even rocks. The best times I remember, though, were when we sang and danced and held prayer meetings.

BRIEN: My favorite thing isn't games either—it's racing horses.

MARCEL, HANNAH, AND SARAH: What?

BRIEN: Since everybody lives so far apart, every summer we have these huge gatherings called rendezvous. Everyone comes from miles around. We have a feast with all my favorite foods. We make bannock, which is a kind of bread, and we have fresh moose, rabbit, and duck. Then I don't have to eat just pemmican.

MARCEL: What's pemmican?

Brien takes some pemmican from his pouch. It resembles beef jerky.

BRIEN: It's just dried meat and salt.

*They all try a bit, except Hannah who looks at it disgustedly and
hands it back to Brien.*

SARAH *(biting into a piece)*: Yuck.

BRIEN: That's what we eat when we hunt and trap because it's easy to carry and it lasts a long time.

HANNAH: I'd like to hear more about the horses.

BRIEN: When everyone is gathered for the rendezvous, we spend a lot of time trading with each other for pots and pans, horses, food, and other things we need. We also trade furs. Once the trading is done, we play games and sing and dance. The women trade their beaded crafts with each other, and the people with fast horses challenge each other to see whose is the fastest. Everyone bets and cheers for their favorite. Those rendezvous are my favorite.

HANNAH: It sounds great, but I wish you hadn't described all that delicious food. I was already hungry and now I'm starving. Let me try some of that pemmican.

Brien hands her some pemmican, which she quickly devours.

BRIEN: Maybe I can catch a rabbit or a deer.

SARAH: Oh, I wish we had some vegetables.

HANNAH: Me, too. Corn or baked sweet potatoes or—

MARCEL: —Pozole with atole.

HANNAH: What's that?

MARCEL: Pozole is a meat stew with vegetables. It's delicious. Atole is something we usually eat in the morning and evening. It's a hot cereal made of ground up and roasted grain. It's kind of mushy, but it's really good.

HANNAH: It sounds kind of like grits.

SARAH: Or oatmeal.

MARCEL: It seems like we eat a lot of things that are almost the same, even though we live so far from each other.

SARAH: Speaking of far from home, are you two staying in a tavern?

BRIEN: Of course not. We set up camp when we travel.

MARCEL: I don't have any money to pay for a room. Sleeping under the stars is free.

SARAH: Couldn't you stay in your carriage?

BRIEN: Ha ha. We don't have carriages, but we do use carts to carry our goods. If we're going across lakes or through rivers, we go by canoe. In the winter we travel by cariole, which is like a sled. It's pulled by a horse or by dogs. It goes quickly over snow.

HANNAH: I've never seen snow.

MARCEL: Neither have I.

SARAH: Even when you travel north?

MARCEL: I've never been away from the mission until now.

HANNAH: Just like I've never been away from the plantation. It's very dangerous to run away. If a slave goes anywhere without permission and gets caught, he's brutally punished. He'll get whipped or worse. I heard of someone who ran away and got hanged for it. That's what I'm afraid of now. That's why I have to get as far north as I can. So I don't get caught.

BRIEN: Gosh.

Read-Aloud Plays: Colonial America • Scholastic Teaching Resources

SARAH: I guess I do have it pretty good. The only things we have to worry about are the cold or disease. Some winters have been so bad that whole colonies have been wiped out.

MARCEL: Wow. I've never experienced cold like that.

SARAH: Our houses are made of wood, but they don't keep out all of the cold.

Brien laughs.

SARAH: What are you laughing at?

BRIEN: I've seen your houses made with boards! Our houses are made of wood, too. But we use the whole tree. Having a cabin made out of thick logs keeps the cold out.

MARCEL: We don't have to keep out the cold—we have to keep out the heat and the rain. Our huts are made of adobe and thatch, a thick grass that keeps the inside from becoming too warm or leaking.

HANNAH: I lived in a wood house, but it was very leaky. It was always either too warm or too cold. We made repairs all the time, but like all the other slave quarters, they weren't built very well to begin with. They're more like wooden boxes than houses. But that's what we were given. These shabby clothes are about all I've ever owned.

SARAH: I can get you some more clothes from home. My parents wouldn't be happy if they knew I was helping a runaway slave, but I think I can take some of my sister's clothes.

HANNAH: Won't she need them?

SARAH: Not the ones she's outgrown. There's a blue dress she just gave to me. It's not a Sunday dress for church, so I don't think anyone will notice. Do you want that one?

HANNAH: Thank you, that's really nice, but you know, I'd go without any clothes if I could go home again.

BRIEN: You'd want to go back to slavery?

HANNAH: No, but I do want to see my family and friends. When I say home, I guess that's what I mean.

SARAH: That's a good way to put it. My house wouldn't be home without the people I love, either.

BRIEN: It sounds like we all miss our homes.

MARCEL: I know what you mean. I didn't like being told what to do by the Spanish padres and soldiers, but I do miss my family and friends, like the rest of you. Maybe I need to forget about where I used to live and start thinking about finding a new home.

SARAH: If home is the place where your friends and family are, perhaps we can all be home just for tonight.

BRIEN: Tomorrow I'll try to find my way back to my family, but tonight, my home is with you.

MARCEL: Home.

HANNAH: Home.

SARAH: Home.

They all laugh and put their arms around each other.

BACKGROUND OF THE DIFFERENT PERSPECTIVES OF THE COLONIES

This play explains some of the similarities and differences among the types of colonies settled by the English, French, and Spanish in North America by presenting a scenario of four children from these colonies meeting for the first time and comparing their lives in those different places and cultures. By the 1760s, these three major European powers had firmly established colonies in the New World. At the time of this play, the English and French had put down their guns to end the French and Indian and Seven Years' wars, but there was still a great deal of animosity between the two countries and their settlements.

During this period, Spain secured its empire in areas of present-day South America, Mexico, and the Southwest United States—south of the areas disputed by the French and British. By 1768, King Charles II of Spain had laid out a plan to establish a string of farms along the present-day California coast to provide an agricultural base for the growth of future cities. Because the Spanish lacked laborers for the farms, they created religious-based farm centers (missions) for which they recruited or coerced Native Americans who lived on the land to work for them in return for food, clothing, and shelter. Those Native Americans who lived and worked on the mission, such as the Yuma mentioned in this play, were forced to accept the Catholic religion, learn Spanish, and adopt many Spanish customs in place of their own. As with enslaved Africans brought to the southern colonies, the suppression of languages and customs caused a tremendous cultural loss.

On the other coast, in the American colonies were thriving and preparing for their war of Independence from Britain. Slavery was an important part of the economy, especially in the South, where agricultural life was made profitable through the widespread use of enslaved African laborers in the plantation system. Although no English colony had officially abolished slavery at this time, many in the New England and some in the Middle Atlantic colonies had simply stopped using slave labor, believing it was morally wrong. Some were even open to Africans owning land and working for their own benefit. This is why most slaves who managed to escape, like Hannah in the play, headed north to the New England colonies or what is now Canada.

In contrast, the Native Americans in North America and the French settlers benefited from a relationship of cultural exchange rather than domination. This was especially true of French trapper colonies, particularly the Métis settlements, which are now parts of Canada and the northern United States. The French who settled these colonies were more open to learning about what the native peoples had to offer and incorporated this learning into their own customs and way of life. Brien's character gives examples of food, clothing, and other blended and borrowed customs in the play.

Notes: The mission from which Marcel's character escapes was probably not well established until the 1790s—after the setting date of this play. Earlier Spanish missions were established in Texas.

You may want to explain to your students that Marcel and Brien would not, in fact, speak English, but would most likely speak Spanish and French, respectively.

PRODUCING THE PLAY

In reading this play in your classroom, it might be best to cast it cross-culturally. Consider having someone of Anglo-American descent play Hannah and someone with a Spanish or Asian background play the French trapper. This way, in explaining the differences in the colonies, each student may gain a better understanding of what each culture, and his or her own culture, may have endured and experienced in the days of early America.

The props required for this play (pouch for Brien, hornbook for Sarah, cotton boll for Hannah, and pack, battledore, and shuttle-cock for Marcel) can be pantomimed or created by students. To see examples of what a battledore and shuttlecock look like, go to http://www.nativetech.org/games/shuttle/. To find an image of a hornbook, check out http://www.iupui.edu/~engwft/hornbook.html. Have students make these props out of craft materials that are already available in the classroom.

For costumes, have students start with what they wear now and find simple ways to alter them to create the looks described by the characters in the play. You might want to add a "fashion show" at the end of the play to give students the chance to describe what they are wearing to the audience and even show some of the other wares mentioned but not worn in the play. On a similar note, you might want to create some of the dishes that are mentioned in the play and pass samples out to the audience.

The children in the play are sitting around a bonfire. A simple (and safe) fire can be made with orange, red, and yellow tissue paper and a small fan. Even a cardboard cut-out of a fire will work. As an acting exercise, have the students pretend that it's cold and they're warming their hands in front of the fire.

WEB LINKS

The Spanish Missions of California.
http://library.thinkquest.org/3615/index.shtml
A kid-friendly, interactive site that explains the history and describes the lives of people who worked on a mission.

Colonial America 1600–1775 Resources.
http://falcon.jmu.edu/~ramseyil/colonial.htm#D0
A great collection of online resources about

the colonial period for students, including links to lesson plans, time lines, information about education, medicine, crafts, and other elements of daily life.

BOOK LINKS

A Mission for the People: The Story of La Purisima by Mary Ann Fraser (Holt, 1998)

The Arrow over the Door by Joseph Bruchac (Dial, 1998) (fiction)

To Be a Slave by Julius Lester (Scholastic, 1988)

Colonial People series by Bobbie Kalman (Crabtree Publishing, 2002)

ACTIVITIES

- ***Compare Four Homes*** This play deals with four different types of settlements in North America. In what ways are they different from each other? In what ways are they similar? Have students make a table that compares and contrasts the four settlements in several of the following categories: food, homes, occupations, education, religion, and chores.

- ***Map an Escape Route From Slavery*** Show students a map of escape routes slaves took to find their way to freedom (the National Park Service provides a simple map online at http://www.nps.gov/boaf/urrmap~1.htm). Encourage them to get a sense of the difficulty of the journey by measuring the distance a runaway slave such as Hannah might have had to travel from a plantation in South Carolina to one of the New England colonies. Set a departure and arrival point for the class and show them how to work with the map scale to measure distance. Then have students walk a mile and time it. They can multiply their time by the number of miles along the route to estimate how long such a journey would take. Be sure they add time for resting and eating.

- *Mission Plan* Have students become familiar with the organization of life on a mission by using graph paper to draw a plan of a mission. They should be sure to include the following elements: quadrangle, church, soldier barracks, Indian village, work area, and fields.

- *Play Ball, Colonial-Style* Have students investigate one of the games mentioned in this play and write a brief summary and list of rules for the game. Visit **http://www. nativetech.org/games/** to learn about the rules of *pokean* and other Native American games. At **http://www.baseball1.com/bbdata/ e-rounders.html** you can find a history of and the rules to the game rounders that Sarah and her friends play. Ask the physical education teacher to help students play the rounders game as their colonial peers might have played it.

NOTES